EMMANUEL JOSEPH

Blueprints of the Divine, Where Medicine, Mythology, and Architecture Converge

Copyright © 2025 by Emmanuel Joseph

All rights reserved. No part of this publication may be reproduced, stored or transmitted in any form or by any means, electronic, mechanical, photocopying, recording, scanning, or otherwise without written permission from the publisher. It is illegal to copy this book, post it to a website, or distribute it by any other means without permission.

First edition

This book was professionally typeset on Reedsy.
Find out more at reedsy.com

Contents

1. Chapter 1: The Seed of Divine Architecture — 1
2. Chapter 2: Healing Through Sacred Spaces — 3
3. Chapter 3: Mythology and the Fabric of Reality — 5
4. Chapter 4: The Alchemical Blueprint — 7
5. Chapter 5: The Sacred Geometry of Healing — 9
6. Chapter 6: The Mythical Guardians of Health — 11
7. Chapter 7: Architectural Alchemy and the Philosopher's Stone — 13
8. Chapter 8: Medicine and the Divine Blueprint — 15
9. Chapter 9: The Architecture of Dreams — 17
10. Chapter 10: Sacred Sites and Healing Rituals — 19
11. Chapter 11: The Convergence of Medicine, Mythology, and... — 21
12. Chapter 12: The Future of Healing Spaces — 23
13. Chapter 13: The Healing Power of Light — 25
14. Chapter 14: The Art of Healing Landscapes — 27
15. Chapter 15: The Symphony of Healing Sounds — 29

1

Chapter 1: The Seed of Divine Architecture

In the earliest dawn of civilization, humans looked to the heavens and crafted structures that reflected their divine visions. Ancient temples, pyramids, and ziggurats stood as testaments to the celestial aspirations of early architects. These monumental structures were not merely places of worship but also embodiments of the divine blueprint that guided the cosmos. From the towering pyramids of Egypt to the intricate temples of Mesopotamia, these edifices encapsulated the mysteries of the universe, merging the celestial with the terrestrial.

These ancient architects were not only builders but also visionaries who understood the profound connection between the human body, the cosmos, and the divine. They believed that by constructing these sacred spaces, they were replicating the universe's divine order on earth. The alignment of these structures with celestial bodies was a testament to their intricate knowledge of astronomy and its significance in their spiritual lives. The very act of building these structures was a form of worship, a way to connect with the divine forces that governed their world.

As centuries passed, the principles of sacred architecture evolved, yet the essence remained the same: to bridge the gap between the mortal and the divine. The Greeks, with their temples dedicated to gods and goddesses, continued this tradition, infusing their structures with a sense of harmony and proportion that mirrored the divine order. The Parthenon, with its precise geometry and alignment, stands as a testament to the Greeks' commitment to embodying divine perfection in their architecture.

In later centuries, this tradition was carried forward by the Romans, who integrated their architectural prowess with the religious and mythological beliefs of their time. The Pantheon, with its awe-inspiring dome and oculus, symbolized the heavens and the divine realm. The Romans believed that by constructing such monumental structures, they were not only honoring their gods but also ensuring the stability and prosperity of their empire. Thus, sacred architecture continued to serve as a bridge between the human and the divine, embodying the spiritual aspirations of civilizations across millennia.

2

Chapter 2: Healing Through Sacred Spaces

The connection between architecture and healing dates back to ancient times when temples served as centers for both spiritual and physical restoration. The concept of healing was not limited to the physical body; it extended to the soul and the mind. Ancient healers and architects understood that the environment played a crucial role in the healing process. This understanding led to the construction of therapeutic spaces designed to harmonize the energies of those seeking solace and recovery.

In ancient Greece, the Asclepieia were temples dedicated to Asclepius, the god of healing. These temples were designed to provide a serene and restorative environment for the sick and the wounded. Patients would undergo a process called 'incubation,' where they would sleep in a sacred area of the temple, hoping to receive divine guidance and healing through their dreams. The architecture of the Asclepieia, with its peaceful courtyards, healing baths, and sacred groves, was meticulously planned to create a therapeutic atmosphere conducive to healing.

Similarly, in ancient Egypt, the temples of Imhotep, the architect and physician who was later deified, served as centers of healing. These temples were not only places of worship but also hospitals where priests practiced medicine and offered remedies derived from natural sources. The design of these temples, with their tranquil gardens and healing sanctuaries, reflected the Egyptians' understanding of the holistic nature of healing, which encompassed the body, mind, and spirit.

The connection between architecture and healing persisted through the ages, influencing the design of medieval monasteries and hospitals. Monastic infirmaries were designed to provide a peaceful and supportive environment for the sick, with gardens, cloisters, and spaces for prayer and meditation. The holistic approach to healing, which integrated spiritual and physical care, continued to shape the design of healing spaces in the modern era, emphasizing the importance of creating environments that nurture and restore.

3

Chapter 3: Mythology and the Fabric of Reality

Mythology has always been a source of inspiration for architects, providing a rich tapestry of symbols and narratives that shape our understanding of the world. The stories of gods, heroes, and mythical creatures have been immortalized in stone, serving as a testament to the enduring power of myth. These myths offer profound insights into the human condition, reflecting our deepest fears, desires, and aspirations.

In ancient Greece, the myths of gods and heroes were intricately woven into the fabric of daily life, influencing everything from art and literature to architecture. The Parthenon, for example, was not merely a temple but a symbolic representation of the triumph of the Athenian state and its patron goddess, Athena. The architectural elements of the Parthenon, including its friezes and sculptures, depicted scenes from mythology, reinforcing the cultural and religious identity of the Athenians.

Similarly, in ancient Rome, mythology played a central role in shaping the architectural landscape. The Romans borrowed heavily from Greek mythology, incorporating the stories of gods and heroes into their own cultural narrative. The Forum of Augustus, with its Temple of Mars Ultor, was a monumental expression of Roman mythology and imperial propaganda. The temple's design and decoration celebrated the divine ancestry of the

Roman emperors and their connection to the gods.

In India, the rich mythology of Hinduism has been a continuous source of inspiration for temple architecture. The intricate carvings and sculptures that adorn the temples are visual representations of the stories from the Puranas and the epics, Ramayana and Mahabharata. These temples serve not only as places of worship but also as repositories of cultural and spiritual knowledge, preserving the myths and legends for future generations.

The influence of mythology on architecture is not confined to the ancient world. In the Gothic cathedrals of medieval Europe, biblical stories and Christian mythology were brought to life through stained glass windows, sculptures, and intricate carvings. These cathedrals were designed to inspire awe and reverence, using the power of myth to convey spiritual truths and moral lessons. The enduring legacy of mythology in architecture underscores its profound impact on our cultural and spiritual consciousness.

4

Chapter 4: The Alchemical Blueprint

The practice of alchemy, with its mystical blend of science, philosophy, and spirituality, has had a profound influence on architecture. Alchemists believed in the transformation of the physical and spiritual realms, a concept that found expression in the design of sacred spaces. The principles of alchemy, including the transformation of base materials into gold and the quest for the philosopher's stone, were mirrored in the architectural designs that sought to embody the divine order and the mysteries of the universe.

In medieval Europe, alchemical symbolism was often incorporated into the design of cathedrals and churches. The intricate carvings, stained glass windows, and architectural details were imbued with alchemical symbols representing transformation, purification, and enlightenment. The labyrinths found in many Gothic cathedrals, for example, symbolized the alchemical journey of the soul towards spiritual enlightenment and union with the divine.

The influence of alchemy extended beyond religious architecture to secular buildings as well. The Renaissance saw a resurgence of interest in alchemy, with many prominent architects incorporating alchemical principles into their designs. The Villa d'Este in Italy, with its elaborate gardens and water features, is a prime example of this fusion of alchemy and architecture. The gardens, designed to represent the alchemical process of transformation, were intended to evoke a sense of wonder and contemplation in visitors.

The Hermetic tradition, which encompasses alchemical thought, also influenced the design of secret societies' meeting places, such as the Freemasons' lodges. These spaces were designed with symbolic elements that reflected the alchemical and Hermetic principles of transformation and enlightenment. The architecture of these lodges, with their carefully planned layouts and symbolic decorations, served as a physical representation of the alchemical journey towards spiritual and intellectual enlightenment.

In modern times, the principles of alchemy continue to inspire architects who seek to create spaces that transcend the physical and connect with the spiritual. The design of contemporary sacred spaces often incorporates elements of alchemical symbolism, reflecting the timeless quest for transformation and enlightenment. The enduring legacy of alchemy in architecture underscores its profound impact on our understanding of the relationship between the physical and spiritual realms.

5

Chapter 5: The Sacred Geometry of Healing

Sacred geometry, with its roots in ancient wisdom, has been a guiding principle in the design of healing spaces. The belief that certain geometric shapes and patterns have inherent healing properties has influenced the architecture of temples, hospitals, and therapeutic centers throughout history. The use of sacred geometry in architecture is based on the understanding that these shapes and patterns resonate with the natural order of the universe, promoting harmony and well-being.

The ancient Egyptians were among the first to incorporate sacred geometry into their architectural designs. The proportions and alignments of the pyramids, for example, were based on geometric principles that reflected the Egyptians' understanding of the cosmos. The Great Pyramid of Giza, with its precise alignment to the cardinal points and its geometric proportions, was believed to be a conduit for spiritual energy and a source of healing.

In ancient Greece, the use of sacred geometry in architecture was closely linked to the concept of harmony and proportion. The Parthenon, with its golden ratio proportions, is a prime example of how the Greeks used geometric principles to create structures that embodied beauty and harmony. The design of healing temples, such as the Asclepieia, also incorporated sacred geometry, with layouts and proportions intended to promote healing and well-being.

The use of sacred geometry in architecture continued through the ages, influencing the design of medieval cathedrals and Renaissance buildings. The Gothic cathedrals of Europe, with their intricate geometric patterns and proportions, were designed to inspire awe and elevate the spirit. The use of sacred geometry in these structures was believed to promote spiritual elevation and healing. The intricate rose windows and labyrinths found in Gothic cathedrals, for example, were based on geometric principles that symbolized the journey of the soul towards enlightenment. These sacred geometric designs were believed to harmonize the energies of the space, creating an environment that fostered spiritual and physical healing.

In the Renaissance, the revival of classical knowledge brought renewed interest in sacred geometry. Architects like Leonardo da Vinci and Filippo Brunelleschi studied the geometric principles underlying ancient structures and incorporated them into their own designs. The use of the golden ratio, symmetry, and proportion in Renaissance architecture reflected a deep understanding of the relationship between geometry and harmony. Buildings designed with these principles were believed to resonate with the natural order of the universe, promoting well-being and balance.

Today, the principles of sacred geometry continue to influence the design of healing spaces. Modern architects and designers draw on these ancient principles to create environments that support physical, mental, and spiritual health. Hospitals, wellness centers, and therapeutic spaces are designed with an understanding of the importance of geometry in promoting healing. The incorporation of natural light, harmonious proportions, and geometric patterns in these spaces reflects the enduring legacy of sacred geometry in the architecture of healing.

6

Chapter 6: The Mythical Guardians of Health

Throughout history, mythology has played a crucial role in shaping our understanding of health and medicine. The stories of mythical guardians and healers have provided inspiration and guidance for both patients and practitioners. These myths often personified the forces of health and illness, offering insights into the nature of disease and the path to healing.

In ancient Greece, Asclepius, the god of medicine, was a central figure in the mythology of healing. The staff of Asclepius, with its single serpent entwined around a rod, remains a symbol of medicine to this day. The temples dedicated to Asclepius were not only places of worship but also centers of healing where patients sought divine intervention for their ailments. The mythology surrounding Asclepius provided a framework for understanding the healing process and the role of the divine in health.

Similarly, in ancient Egypt, the goddess Sekhmet was revered as a powerful healer and protector against disease. Her mythological role as a fierce lioness and a compassionate healer embodied the dual nature of health and illness. Temples dedicated to Sekhmet were centers of healing, where priests and healers invoked her protection and guidance in their medical practices. The mythology of Sekhmet provided a symbolic framework for understanding the balance between health and illness and the role of divine intervention in healing.

In India, the mythological figure of Dhanvantari, the divine physician, is revered as the god of Ayurveda, the ancient system of medicine. According to Hindu mythology, Dhanvantari emerged from the ocean of milk during the churning of the ocean, carrying a pot of amrita, the nectar of immortality. He is depicted holding a conch, a discus, and a pot of healing herbs, symbolizing his role as the divine healer. The mythology of Dhanvantari continues to inspire Ayurvedic practitioners and patients, providing a spiritual context for the practice of holistic medicine.

The influence of mythology on health and medicine is not limited to the ancient world. In medieval Europe, the saints and martyrs associated with healing, such as Saint Roch and Saint Blaise, played a significant role in the religious and medical practices of the time. Their stories and symbols were invoked in prayers and rituals for healing and protection. The enduring legacy of these mythical guardians of health reflects the deep connection between mythology, medicine, and the human quest for healing.

7

Chapter 7: Architectural Alchemy and the Philosopher's Stone

The quest for the philosopher's stone, a mythical substance believed to grant immortality and transform base metals into gold, has long fascinated alchemists and architects alike. The principles of alchemy, with its focus on transformation and transmutation, have influenced architectural design in profound ways. The search for the philosopher's stone can be seen as a metaphor for the pursuit of perfection and enlightenment in both architecture and the human spirit.

In medieval Europe, the practice of alchemy was closely linked to the design of sacred spaces. Alchemical symbols and principles were often incorporated into the architecture of churches and cathedrals, reflecting the belief in the transformative power of the divine. The alchemical process of purification and transformation was symbolized in the design of these structures, with elements such as the labyrinth and the rose window representing the journey of the soul towards enlightenment.

The Renaissance brought a renewed interest in alchemy and its influence on architecture. Architects like Leon Battista Alberti and Andrea Palladio drew on alchemical principles in their designs, seeking to create buildings that embodied harmony, proportion, and perfection. The use of geometric principles, symmetry, and proportion in Renaissance architecture reflected the alchemical belief in the underlying order and harmony of the universe. Buildings designed with these principles were intended to inspire awe and elevate the spirit, mirroring the alchemical quest for transformation and enlightenment.

In the modern era, the principles of alchemy continue to inspire architects who seek to create transformative and transcendent spaces. The design of contemporary sacred spaces often incorporates alchemical symbols and principles, reflecting the timeless quest for the philosopher's stone. These spaces are designed to promote healing, enlightenment, and spiritual transformation, embodying the alchemical process of turning base materials into gold. The enduring influence of alchemy on architecture underscores its profound impact on our understanding of the relationship between the physical and spiritual realms.

8

Chapter 8: Medicine and the Divine Blueprint

The connection between medicine and the divine blueprint has been a central theme in the history of healing practices. Ancient healers often believed that the human body was a microcosm of the universe, governed by the same divine principles that shaped the cosmos. This understanding influenced the development of medical practices and the design of healing spaces, as practitioners sought to align their work with the divine order.

In ancient Greece, the Hippocratic tradition emphasized the importance of harmony and balance in health. The principles of the Hippocratic Oath, which continue to guide medical ethics today, were based on the belief in the divine blueprint that governed the human body and the natural world. Hippocratic physicians sought to restore balance in the body through natural remedies and treatments, reflecting the understanding that health was a state of harmony with the divine order.

Similarly, in traditional Chinese medicine, the concept of the Tao, or the Way, emphasized the importance of aligning one's life with the natural and cosmic order. The practice of acupuncture, herbal medicine, and other traditional therapies was based on the understanding that the human body was a reflection of the universe, governed by the same principles of balance and harmony. The design of healing spaces, such as traditional Chinese medicine clinics, reflected this understanding, with a focus on creating environments that promoted balance and well-being.

In Ayurvedic medicine, the ancient system of healing from India, the concept of the divine blueprint is central to the understanding of health and disease. According to Ayurveda, the human body is governed by the doshas, or fundamental energies, which reflect the underlying principles of the universe. Ayurvedic practitioners seek to restore balance in the body through diet, lifestyle, and herbal remedies, reflecting the belief in the divine order that governs health and well-being. The design of Ayurvedic clinics and healing centers often incorporates elements of sacred geometry and natural materials, reflecting the holistic approach to healing.

The connection between medicine and the divine blueprint continues to shape modern healing practices. Integrative and holistic medicine, which emphasizes the importance of treating the whole person, draws on the ancient understanding of the human body as a microcosm of the universe. The design of contemporary healing spaces often reflects this understanding, with a focus on creating environments that promote harmony and balance. The enduring influence of the divine blueprint on medicine underscores its profound impact on our understanding of health and healing.

9

Chapter 9: The Architecture of Dreams

The architecture of dreams has long fascinated both architects and dreamers, offering a glimpse into the subconscious mind and the realm of the divine. Dreams have been a source of inspiration for architectural design, providing a window into the imaginative and the surreal. The connection between architecture and dreams reflects the belief in the power of the subconscious to shape our understanding of the world and our place in it.

In ancient Egypt, dreams were considered a means of communication with the divine. The temples of Imhotep, the architect and physician who was later deified, served as centers for dream incubation, where individuals sought divine guidance and healing through their dreams. The architecture of these temples, with their serene and tranquil environments, was designed to facilitate the dream experience, reflecting the belief in the power of dreams to connect with the divine.

In ancient Greece, the practice of dream incubation was also central to the healing temples of Asclepius. Patients would sleep in a sacred area of the temple, hoping to receive divine guidance and healing through their dreams. The architecture of these temples, with their peaceful courtyards, healing baths, and sacred groves, was designed to create an environment conducive to dreaming and spiritual revelation. The connection between dreams and healing was an integral part of the ancient Greek understanding of health and well-being.

The influence of dreams on architecture is not limited to the ancient world. In the 20th century, the Surrealist movement sought to explore the architecture of dreams, creating imaginative and fantastical designs that reflected the subconscious mind. Architects like Antoni Gaudí and Salvador Dalí drew on dream imagery to create buildings that defied conventional norms and challenged the boundaries of reality. The dreamlike quality of their designs reflected the belief in the power of the imagination to transform the built environment.

In contemporary architecture, the influence of dreams continues to inspire innovative and imaginative designs. Architects and designers draw on the imagery and symbolism of dreams to create spaces that evoke a sense of wonder and transcendence. The architecture of dreams reminds us of the profound connection between our subconscious mind and the spaces we inhabit. Modern architects explore innovative materials, fluid forms, and imaginative designs to create dreamlike environments that resonate with the inner world of the dreamer. These spaces invite us to step beyond the boundaries of reality and engage with the mystical and surreal aspects of our consciousness.

The creation of immersive, dream-inspired spaces can be seen in the design of contemporary museums, art installations, and interactive experiences. These environments draw on the power of dreams to evoke emotions, provoke thought, and inspire creativity. The integration of light, color, and form in these spaces reflects the fluid and ever-changing nature of dreams, encouraging visitors to explore new dimensions of perception and imagination.

As we continue to explore the architecture of dreams, we are reminded of the enduring power of the subconscious to shape our understanding of the world. The spaces we inhabit, whether in reality or in dreams, reflect our deepest desires, fears, and aspirations. By embracing the architecture of dreams, we can create environments that inspire, heal, and transform, bridging the gap between the conscious and the subconscious, the mundane and the divine.

10

Chapter 10: Sacred Sites and Healing Rituals

Throughout history, sacred sites have served as centers of healing and spiritual transformation. These places, often imbued with natural beauty and mystical significance, have drawn pilgrims seeking physical and spiritual rejuvenation. The architecture of these sacred sites reflects the deep connection between the natural world and the divine, providing a setting for rituals and practices that promote healing and well-being.

One of the most renowned sacred sites in the world is Stonehenge in England. This ancient stone circle has long been associated with healing and spiritual rituals. Archaeological evidence suggests that people traveled great distances to Stonehenge seeking cures for their ailments, and the site may have been used as a center for healing ceremonies. The precise alignment of the stones with celestial bodies adds to the site's mystical allure, reinforcing its role as a place of spiritual significance.

In ancient Greece, the sanctuary of Epidaurus was another important center for healing. The sanctuary, dedicated to Asclepius, the god of medicine, was renowned for its healing rituals and therapies. Pilgrims would undergo a process of purification before entering the sanctuary, where they would participate in rituals and receive treatments from the priests. The architecture of Epidaurus, with its peaceful temples, healing baths, and sacred groves, was designed to create a therapeutic environment conducive to healing.

In India, the sacred city of Varanasi on the banks of the Ganges River has long been revered as a place of spiritual and physical healing. Pilgrims come to Varanasi to bathe in the holy waters of the Ganges, seeking purification and healing. The ghats, or steps leading down to the river, are lined with temples and shrines, creating a sacred architectural landscape that reflects the city's spiritual significance. The rituals and ceremonies performed at Varanasi are believed to cleanse the soul and promote well-being.

The connection between sacred sites and healing rituals continues to be a powerful force in the modern world. Many people visit ancient and contemporary sacred sites seeking spiritual and physical rejuvenation. The architecture of these sites, with their emphasis on natural beauty, harmony, and spirituality, provides a setting for rituals and practices that promote healing and transformation. The enduring legacy of sacred sites and healing rituals underscores their profound impact on our understanding of the relationship between the natural world, the divine, and human health.

11

Chapter 11: The Convergence of Medicine, Mythology, and Architecture

The convergence of medicine, mythology, and architecture has shaped our understanding of health and healing throughout history. These three fields, each with its own unique principles and practices, have intersected in ways that reflect the holistic nature of human well-being. The integration of medicine, mythology, and architecture has provided a framework for understanding the complex interplay between the physical, mental, and spiritual aspects of health.

In ancient civilizations, the practice of medicine was deeply intertwined with mythology and architecture. Healers and architects worked together to create therapeutic spaces that reflected the divine order and promoted healing. The temples of Asclepius in Greece and the healing sanctuaries of Egypt are prime examples of this convergence, where architecture and mythology played a crucial role in the healing process.

The Renaissance saw a renewed interest in the integration of medicine, mythology, and architecture. The revival of classical knowledge and the principles of harmony and proportion influenced the design of healing spaces. Architects like Andrea Palladio drew on these principles to create buildings that embodied the ideals of beauty, balance, and health. The use of geometric principles and natural materials in Renaissance architecture reflected the understanding that the built environment could promote physical and spiritual well-being.

In the modern era, the convergence of medicine, mythology, and architecture continues to shape our understanding of health and healing. Integrative and holistic approaches to medicine emphasize the importance of treating the whole person, recognizing the interconnectedness of the physical, mental, and spiritual aspects of health. The design of contemporary healing spaces reflects this understanding, with an emphasis on creating environments that promote harmony, balance, and well-being.

The enduring legacy of the convergence of medicine, mythology, and architecture underscores its profound impact on our understanding of health and healing. By integrating these fields, we can create spaces that support physical, mental, and spiritual well-being, reflecting the holistic nature of human health. The principles and practices that have emerged from this convergence continue to inspire and guide us as we seek to promote healing and well-being in the modern world.

12

Chapter 12: The Future of Healing Spaces

As we look to the future, the principles of medicine, mythology, and architecture will continue to shape the design of healing spaces. Advances in technology, materials, and design will provide new opportunities to create environments that support physical, mental, and spiritual well-being. The integration of these fields will enable us to create spaces that are not only functional but also inspiring, promoting health and healing in innovative ways.

One of the key trends shaping the future of healing spaces is the use of biophilic design, which emphasizes the connection between humans and nature. Incorporating natural elements such as plants, water features, and natural light into the design of healing spaces can promote well-being and reduce stress. Biophilic design principles can be applied to hospitals, wellness centers, and therapeutic spaces, creating environments that support healing and rejuvenation.

The use of technology in the design of healing spaces will also play a significant role in the future. Advances in materials and construction techniques will enable architects to create innovative and sustainable buildings that promote health and well-being. Smart technologies, such as sensors and interactive systems, can enhance the functionality and comfort of healing spaces, providing personalized environments that cater to individual needs.

The integration of mythology and storytelling in the design of healing spaces will continue to inspire and engage us. The use of symbolic elements, narratives, and artwork can create environments that resonate with the human spirit, providing a sense of meaning and connection. By drawing on the rich tapestry of myths and legends, architects and designers can create spaces that inspire awe, wonder, and healing.

The future of healing spaces lies in the continued convergence of medicine, mythology, and architecture. By embracing the principles and practices of these fields, we can create environments that support holistic well-being and reflect the interconnectedness of the physical, mental, and spiritual aspects of health. As we move forward, the legacy of this convergence will continue to inspire and guide us, shaping the future of healing spaces and promoting health and well-being for generations to come.

13

Chapter 13: The Healing Power of Light

Light has always played a vital role in architecture and healing, symbolizing knowledge, purity, and divine presence. Throughout history, architects have harnessed the healing power of light to create spaces that inspire awe and promote well-being. The interplay of natural light and architectural design has the ability to transform spaces, creating environments that nurture the body, mind, and spirit.

In ancient Egypt, the architecture of temples was designed to capture and manipulate natural light. The alignment of temples with the sun's path and the use of strategically placed openings created dramatic effects, illuminating sacred spaces and enhancing their spiritual significance. The temple of Abu Simbel, for example, was designed so that on certain days of the year, the rising sun would penetrate the sanctuary and illuminate the statues of the gods, symbolizing the divine presence.

The Gothic cathedrals of medieval Europe also exemplify the use of light in architecture to create a sense of the divine. The soaring stained glass windows, with their intricate designs and vibrant colors, filtered light into the cathedrals, creating a mesmerizing play of light and shadow. This use of light was intended to inspire awe and elevate the spirit, reinforcing the connection between the physical and the divine. The use of light in these sacred spaces was believed to have a healing effect on the soul, promoting spiritual well-being.

In modern architecture, the use of light continues to play a central role in the design of healing spaces. Hospitals, wellness centers, and therapeutic environments are designed to maximize natural light, creating bright and welcoming spaces that promote health and well-being. The incorporation of large windows, skylights, and light wells helps to connect indoor spaces with the natural world, fostering a sense of harmony and balance. The use of light in these spaces reflects the enduring belief in its healing power and its ability to transform the built environment.

The integration of light and architecture in healing spaces is also evident in the design of contemporary sacred spaces. Architects draw on the principles of sacred geometry and natural light to create environments that inspire contemplation and spiritual reflection. The use of light to highlight architectural details and create a sense of movement and flow enhances the spiritual experience, promoting a sense of connection with the divine. The healing power of light continues to shape the design of spaces that nurture the body, mind, and spirit.

14

Chapter 14: The Art of Healing Landscapes

The design of healing landscapes has long been a central aspect of architecture and medicine. The integration of natural elements such as gardens, water features, and green spaces into the built environment promotes physical, mental, and spiritual well-being. Healing landscapes provide a setting for relaxation, reflection, and rejuvenation, creating environments that support the holistic nature of health and healing.

The ancient Persians were among the first to recognize the therapeutic potential of gardens, designing lush, walled paradises known as "paradeisos." These gardens were designed to evoke the harmony and beauty of the natural world, providing a serene retreat from the stresses of daily life. The use of water features, fragrant plants, and shaded walkways created a sensory experience that promoted relaxation and well-being.

In ancient Greece, the concept of the healing garden was also central to the design of therapeutic spaces. The Asclepieia, dedicated to the god of healing, often included serene gardens where patients could rest and recuperate. The integration of natural elements such as trees, flowers, and water features into the design of these healing sanctuaries reflected the belief in the restorative power of nature. The gardens provided a tranquil setting for patients to connect with the natural world, promoting physical and emotional healing.

The tradition of healing landscapes continued through the ages, influencing the design of medieval monasteries and hospitals. Monastic gardens were designed to provide a peaceful and supportive environment for the sick and infirm, with medicinal plants and herbs used for healing remedies. The integration of gardens, cloisters, and green spaces into the design of monastic infirmaries reflected the holistic approach to healing, which emphasized the importance of the natural environment in promoting health and well-being.

In the modern era, the principles of healing landscapes continue to shape the design of therapeutic environments. Hospitals, rehabilitation centers, and wellness facilities incorporate gardens, rooftop green spaces, and healing terraces into their design, creating environments that support recovery and well-being. The use of natural elements, such as plants, water features, and outdoor seating areas, provides patients with a sense of connection to the natural world, promoting relaxation and healing. The enduring legacy of healing landscapes underscores their profound impact on our understanding of the relationship between nature, architecture, and health.

15

Chapter 15: The Symphony of Healing Sounds

Sound has always played a significant role in architecture and healing, with its ability to influence emotions, mood, and well-being. The use of sound in the design of healing spaces reflects the understanding that auditory experiences can have a profound impact on the body and mind. From the harmonious chants of ancient temples to the soothing sounds of modern therapeutic environments, sound has been harnessed to create spaces that promote healing and tranquility.

In ancient cultures, sound was often used in religious and healing rituals to create a sense of connection with the divine. The chanting of hymns, the ringing of bells, and the playing of musical instruments were integral to the spiritual practices of ancient civilizations. The architecture of temples and sacred spaces was designed to enhance the acoustics, creating an environment where the sounds of worship could resonate and inspire. The use of sound in these spaces was believed to have a healing effect on the soul, promoting spiritual well-being.

The ancient Greeks also recognized the therapeutic potential of sound, incorporating music and rhythm into their healing practices. The philosopher Pythagoras believed in the healing power of music, using harmonic frequencies to treat physical and emotional ailments. The design of Greek theaters and healing sanctuaries reflected this understanding, with acoustics carefully planned to amplify the therapeutic sounds of music and chants. The integration of sound into the architectural design of these spaces created an environment conducive to healing and relaxation.

In the medieval period, the use of sound in architecture continued to play a central role in the design of sacred spaces. The soaring vaults and arches of Gothic cathedrals were designed to enhance the acoustics, allowing the sounds of choir chants and organ music to fill the space with resonance and beauty. The use of sound in these sacred spaces was intended to elevate the spirit and create a sense of awe and reverence. The connection between sound and architecture in these spaces reflected the belief in the healing power of auditory experiences.

In contemporary architecture, the use of sound continues to shape the design of healing environments. Hospitals, wellness centers, and therapeutic spaces often incorporate elements of sound therapy, such as soothing music, water features, and nature sounds, to create a calming atmosphere. The careful planning of acoustics in these spaces ensures that the auditory experience promotes relaxation and well-being. The integration of sound into the design of healing environments reflects the enduring belief in its therapeutic potential and its ability to transform the built environment.

Book Description:

Blueprints of the Divine: Where Medicine, Mythology, and Architecture Converge explores the profound intersections between three seemingly distinct fields: medicine, mythology, and architecture. This captivating journey delves into the ancient wisdom and modern innovations that have shaped our understanding of health, healing, and the built environment. Through twelve richly detailed chapters, the book examines the sacred spaces, healing rituals, and symbolic designs that have inspired and guided civilizations throughout history.

From the majestic temples of ancient Egypt to the harmonious cathedrals of medieval Europe, and from the holistic healing sanctuaries of Greece to the therapeutic landscapes of the modern era, **Blueprints of the Divine** reveals the timeless principles that continue to influence the architecture of

CHAPTER 15: THE SYMPHONY OF HEALING SOUNDS

healing. The book explores the role of light, sound, sacred geometry, and natural elements in creating environments that promote physical, mental, and spiritual well-being. It also delves into the myths and legends that have provided a symbolic framework for understanding health and disease, offering insights into the human quest for transformation and enlightenment.

With its engaging narrative and deep insights, **Blueprints of the Divine** is a celebration of the holistic nature of health and healing. It invites readers to explore the profound connections between the physical and the spiritual, the ancient and the modern, and the human and the divine. Whether you are an architect, a healer, a student of mythology, or simply someone seeking inspiration, this book offers a rich tapestry of knowledge and wisdom that will deepen your appreciation for the sacred art of healing.